KU-709-661

Communicating Today

Newspapers

Chris Oxlade

Heinemann LIBRARY

www.heinemann.co.uk/library
Visit our website to find out more information about **Heinemann Library** books.

To order:
 Phone ++44 (0)1865 888066
Send a fax to ++44 (0)1865 314091
 Visit the Heinemann Bookshop at www.heinemann.co.uk/library to browse our catalogue and order online.

First published in Great Britain by Heinemann Library, Halley Court, Jordan Hill, Oxford OX2 8EJ, a division of Reed Educational and Professional Publishing Ltd. Heinemann is a registered trademark of Reed Educational & Professional Publishing Ltd.

OXFORD MELBOURNE AUCKLAND JOHANNESBURG BLANTYRE
GABORONE IBADAN PORTSMOUTH NH (USA) CHICAGO

© Reed Educational and Professional Publishing Ltd 2001
The moral right of the proprietor has been asserted.

Designed by Visual Image
Illustrations by Visual Image
Originated by Ambassador Litho Ltd.
Printed in Hong Kong/China

05 04 03 02 01
10 9 8 7 6 5 4 3 2 1
ISBN 0431 11370 X

British Library Cataloguing in Publication Data

Oxlade, Chris
  Newspapers. – (Communicating today)
  1. Newspapers – Juvenile literature
  I. Title
  070.1'72

Acknowledgements

The Publishers would like to thank the following for permission to reproduce photographs: *The Age*: p17; Corbis: pp6, 8, 9, 22, 23, 27, 28, Gail Mooney p13; *Daily Mirror*: p29; Eye Ubiquitous: p25; *Financial Times*: p21; United States Department of Agriculture Animal and Plant Health Inspection Service Legislative and Public Affairs: p17; Impact: p11; *International Herald Tribune*: p26; PA News Photo: pp10, 12; Photodisc: pp4, 5; Raymond Gubbay: p17; Sainsbury's: p17; Sheena Verdun-Taylor: pp15, 18, 20, 24; Stone/Bruce Ayres: p16; Tudor Photography: p14.

Cover photograph reproduced with permission of Corbis.

Every effort has been made to contact copyright holders of any material reproduced in this book. Any omissions will be rectified in subsequent printings if notice is given to the Publisher.

CONTENTS

Any words appearing in the text in bold, **like this**, are explained in the Glossary.

WHAT ARE COMMUNICATIONS?

Communications are ways of sending and receiving information. Important ones include television, radio, telephone (and fax), the **Internet** (and **e-mail**), post and newspapers.

This book is about newspapers. It examines how news is collected and turned into stories, how newspapers are produced and printed, and how they get from the newspapers' offices to homes, shops and news stands. It looks at the technology and science used, and the people involved in the industry.

For many people, reading the newspaper is an important daily routine. It keeps them up-to-date with events in the world and helps to pass the time on the way to work.

Making a newspaper

Every day, hundreds of millions of people buy a newspaper to read about what is happening in the world. Newspapers give us news about events, business, politics, sport, science and technology both in our own countries and abroad. They also provide information about the weather, travel and television programmes. In a newspaper, there is space for lengthy discussion of the news, too, for which there is no time in most television and radio news bulletins.

This book will explain how a typical national daily newspaper is created and **distributed**. Starting at the beginning of one day, it looks at what happens at the paper's offices during that day, ending with the newspaper being produced and distributed overnight, ready to be bought by readers the following day.

This is a small selection of the thousands of newspapers printed throughout the world. It includes daily and weekly papers, national and international newspapers and specialist sports papers.

PUBLISHING NEWSPAPERS

Publishing is the process of making information available for the public to read or look at. More than 6000 different daily newspaper titles are published in North America, Asia and Europe. They cover local, regional, national and international news stories on dozens of different subjects.

Many newspapers are published in different **editions**, each a few hours apart, with each edition containing the latest news. Many have weekend editions that cover the week's news in more detail as well. Some companies and trade organizations also publish their own weekly or monthly newspapers.

The number of copies of a newspaper that are printed (called the **print run**) depends on the type of paper and how many people buy it. A local paper might have a print run of 10,000, while a national newspaper might have a print run of several million.

In some countries, such as China, newspapers are posted on boards called news walls for people to read. Many people cannot afford to buy a paper for themselves.

From story to paper

Typical news stories might be about what a country's government is doing, or a disaster such as a fire. Reporters investigate these events and write about them. The words they write are called **copy**. A photographer takes photographs of the events. The copy and photographs, adverts, and other elements, such as a weather forecast, are gathered together and a **page layout** is decided. When all the pages are filled, the newspaper is printed and **distributed** to its readers.

Newspaper departments

- The editorial department gathers news, writes copy, selects photographs and organizes how the pages will look.
- The production department is responsible for printing and distributing the newspaper.
- The advertising department sells the advertising space in the newspaper and collects the adverts for each edition.
- The accounts department collects money from advertisers and newspaper sellers.

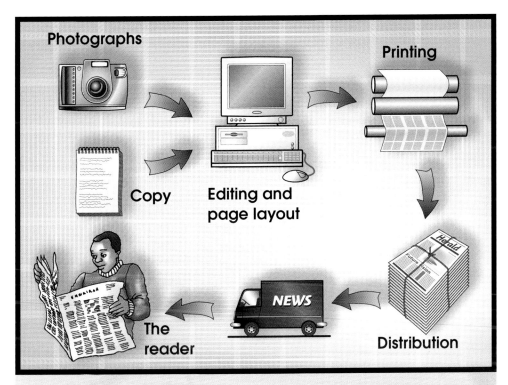

This diagram shows you how a newspaper is put together, printed and published. Different people are involved at each stage, all working to tight deadlines.

GATHERING THE NEWS

Most of the news stories that you read in a newspaper are written by the newspaper's own reporters, who are called staff reporters. Some are general reporters, who cover a wide range of stories, and some are specialist reporters, who might just cover stories about crime or education, for example.

As soon as a new story happens, or **breaks**, a news **editor**, who works at the paper's newsroom, decides whether to send a reporter and photographer to the scene.

News of an event such as a fire might reach the newsroom at midday. A reporter and photographer are sent to the scene. The reporter's job is to decide what the newspaper's readers will be interested in, and interview the people involved (such as those evacuated, or members of the emergency services). He or she uses a word processor on a computer, or a notebook to note the facts, and a tape recorder to record interviews.

Newspaper reporters and photographers, along with journalists from television stations, gathered at the scene of a news story. They may have to wait for hours to get their story.

The newspaper reporter's main tools are a portable tape recorder for recording interviews and a notebook for writing down facts. Later she will write the story on a word processor.

Many events that newspapers cover, such as weddings and public meetings, are known about before they happen. They are known as diary jobs because details of them are kept in a dairy so that they are not missed. The news editor decides whether to send a reporter to them.

Feature writers

Not all the stories in a newspaper contain the latest news. Some look at the previous day's news in more detail. Others are about a particular subject, such as fashion or motoring, and appear every day or every week. These are called **features**, and they are written by feature writers. Other sections of the newspaper include readers' letters and the 'editorial', which is written by the editor-in-chief.

News agencies

News agencies, such as the famous Reuters agency, are an important source of stories. They supply stories to newspapers, who pay the agencies in return. Many newspapers use agencies to get details of international stories which they cannot cover themselves because they do not have reporters working around the world.

EDITING THE COPY

Reporters write **copy** for the story at the scene of the event, using a word processor on a portable computer. When it is complete, they **upload**, or send, the file to the computer in the newspaper's newsroom using a **modem** and telephone. The file can go either along a direct phone line, or by **e-mail** through the **Internet**.

Which stories?

News stories arrive in the newsroom throughout the day and night. News **editors** read them and decide which ones to put in the next day's newspaper. For example, copy for a story about a major fire might arrive in the newsroom in the middle of the afternoon. The editor feels that readers are interested in disaster stories, and that it could provide the chance to use a dramatic photograph, so decides that it should be printed.

The other sections (parts) of the newspaper (such as sports and **features**) have their own editors who decide what to include in their sections. The editor-in-chief is responsible for the whole newspaper and its contents.

This reporter is using a satellite telephone system to send a report and photographs from his computer in the Himalayas in Nepal to his office in London.

Newspaper journalists have to work quickly to get their copy ready to go into the newspaper. They may have to work very long hours if a major story breaks.

Editing

The copy from reporters cannot be put straight on to the newspaper's pages. It has to be **edited** by a sub-editor first. The sub-editor's job is to check that a story is accurate in every way and that it reads well. Sub-editors also cut the text to fit the space available on the page without leaving out important details. They may have to make up a headline for the story that will catch the reader's interest.

Checking the facts

Newspaper stories contain the names of people and places, dates and **statistics**. These must be carefully checked to make sure that all spellings and numbers are correct. Reporters use reference books such as dictionaries and atlases, **on-line** reference material stored on the newspaper's computer, and the Internet. They can also look at old copies of the newspaper that are stored in an **archive**.

NEWSPAPER PICTURES

Newspapers use pictures as well as words. A good photograph can give more information about a story than hundreds of words. It can show the actual scene of a story, or the people involved. It can give vital information, or simply attract the reader to the story in the first place. In some sections of the paper, such as the fashion section, the pictures are as important as the words. For some stories, diagrams or maps drawn on a computer help readers understand the information better.

Digital photographs

Usually, staff (the newspaper's own) photographers sent to the scene of a story take photographs with a **digital** camera. It records the photographs in computer **memory** rather than on normal photographic film.

A news photographer sending photographs back to his office via mobile phone. He has just taken the photographs on a digital camera and checked them on a portable computer.

The photographer **downloads** the photographs from the camera on to a portable computer, where he or she checks that they show what is wanted and are technically sound (for example, that they are in focus). Then they **upload** them through the telephone network to a computer called an **electronic picture desk** at the newspaper office. Here, the picture **editor** can look at them. A photographer sends in several photographs that might be suitable to go with a story.

More photo sources

News stories are also covered by **freelance** photographers and photograph agencies. They send their photographs to the electronic picture desks of all the main newspapers. Sometimes a photograph of a famous person or place is needed for a story. The picture editor searches for suitable photographs on the computer, where there is a **database** containing millions of photographs. Photographs can also be taken electronically from live television or video pictures.

Selecting a part of a photograph to print is called cropping. The boxes show two possible crops of this photograph that would make good pictures.

NEWSPAPER DESIGN

Every newspaper has its own 'look'. Its pages are designed differently, it has letters that are different shapes and sizes, and different ways of laying out its stories. Most important is the newspaper's name on the front page, called the title. It is large and clear so that people can easily identify the newspaper on a news stand.

Newspaper pages are divided into upright strips called columns. There are normally between six and twelve columns across a page. Stories run down the columns and then from one column to the next. The narrow columns are designed to make the stories easy to read without losing your place.

The newspaper is divided into sections, such as national news, international news, sports, business, science and technology, and stories are sorted into these sections. Each section always appears in the same place on the same page so that readers know where to look for stories they are interested in.

Different newspapers attract different readers. The design of a newspaper affects how interesting or exciting it looks.

Page layout

The contents of a paper are planned by the section **editors** several days in advance. They draw a plan called a **flat plan** which shows each page in miniature. Spaces are left for news stories. In the late afternoon the section editors decide where the day's news stories are going to go in the next day's newspaper. They also choose a story for the front page.

Copy, pictures and adverts are put on the pages by sub-editors and designers using computers. As soon as stories, **features** and adverts are ready, they are sent to the **page layout** computers, where they are put in place. The computer automatically arranges the copy into its columns, and turns it into the right typeface and size. A story such as a natural disaster, together with a dramatic photograph, might be chosen for the top of page 2. It could be in place, with its photograph, by early evening.

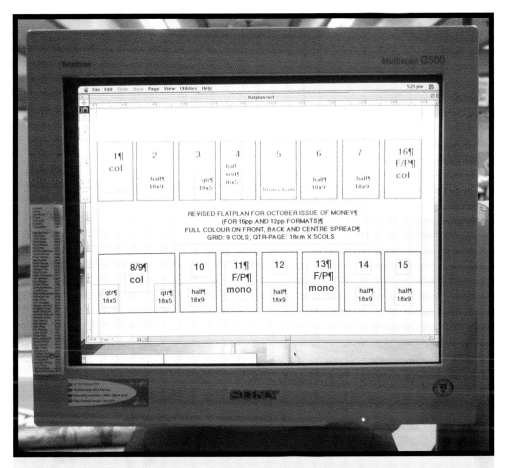

This is a flat plan seen on screen. Laying out each page like this helps editors decide what they want to put in the paper.

ADVERTISING

Up to half the space in a newspaper is taken up by adverts. Advertising is the main method of making money for most newspapers. Throughout the day, people in the advertising department try to fill the newspaper's advertising space. Some take details from readers who phone in with their adverts. Others phone companies to try to persuade them to put adverts in the paper. All the adverts for the next day's newspaper must be ready by the middle of the afternoon.

Types of advert

Display adverts are individual adverts, normally placed by large companies. They are designed to attract the reader's attention, using words, photographs or pictures. Display adverts can appear on any page of the newspaper. Many companies ask for their adverts to be placed well away from unpleasant stories or shocking photographs, in case these affect the positive 'image' of their business that they want to create.

There is a great deal of space to be filled by adverts in each day's paper. Selling that space is easier if the paper itself is selling well, but it is still a difficult job.

Classified adverts are small adverts that are arranged in groups under different headings. They are placed by small companies and readers who want to advertise things like holidays, houses for rent, and articles for sale.

Some, especially local, newspapers can contain hundreds or thousands of individual classified adverts. The adverts are received by post, by phone, by **e-mail** and from the newspaper's **website**. A computer automatically organizes them into the columns reserved for them.

Paying for advertising

The fee that a newspaper charges for placing an advert depends on how much space the advert takes up. The larger the advert, the higher the fee. An advert a few lines long in the classified section will not cost much. An advert that takes up half a page will cost considerably more. Adverts filling the front or back covers cost much more again because they are more likely to be seen by the readers.

Adverts must attract the reader into reading them if they are to make money. The adverts seen here include large display adverts and small classified ones.

PREPARING TO PRINT

Newspapers are printed on huge **printing presses**, often in the same building as the newspaper offices. On the press, the letters, photographs and **graphics** (such as maps or diagrams) on the pages are made by pressing black and coloured inks on to blank paper. The pattern that the inks make is created by flexible aluminium **printing plates**. The first stage in printing an **edition** of a newspaper is to make these printing plates.

Making plates

A printing plate for each page of the newspaper is made from the finished pages stored by **editors** on the **page layout** computer. Plates are made in the plate-making area of the printing department, using special laser printers and photographic processes. Before the printing plates are made, a copy of each page, called a **proof**, is printed out on a colour printer to check that everything looks right.

Printing plates (bottom) and the film (top) that they were made from. A printing plate is made by laying film over a blank plate and exposing it to light.

Late additions

By the middle of evening, printing plates for most of the pages of a daily newspaper have been made. There are still gaps on some pages; these are being kept for evening events, such as reports from sporting fixtures, or reviews of plays at the theatre. This **copy** must be **edited** and put into the gaps left for it by about midnight at the latest. Once it is in place, the plates of these pages are made in about half an hour. Only then can the printing of the next morning's paper begin.

Evening newspapers are often published in several editions during the afternoon and evening, with the latest news in each one. There is a cut-off time for each edition, when all the pages must be ready for their plates to be made. Some plates stay the same for each edition, but others need changing.

Dots for photos

If you look at a photograph in a newspaper with a magnifying glass, you will see that it is made up of tiny dots. Some are black, others are magenta (red), cyan (blue) or yellow. Dots of different sizes and in different proportions make different colours and shades, creating an image. A computer works out how big to make each dot on the printing plates for each photograph in the newspaper.

Photographs and other pictures are printed as tiny dots, as shown by this magnified photograph. The larger the dots, the darker the area of the photo looks.

PRINTING

A newspaper **printing press** is a massive machine, around the same size as a small house. Huge rolls of blank paper go in at one end and finished newspapers come out of the other end. Each newspaper takes just a few seconds to print.

Plates in place

Before printing starts, the **printing plates** are put in the press. Most presses have several **printing units**. Some units print just in black (called mono units) and some print in colour. In each printing unit, the printing plates are attached to large cylinders. Mono units have one cylinder. Colour units have four cylinders, one for each colour that makes up the final images. These colours are normally cyan (blue), magenta (red), yellow and black. The **page layout** computers divide the colours on coloured pages into their cyan, magenta, yellow and black parts, and four plates are made, one for each colour.

Each cylinder carries up to sixteen printing plates, wrapped around the cylinder, normally in two rows of eight pages.

This is a plate cylinder on a rotary printing press. Flexible printing plates are attached side-by-side on the cylinder.

Offset printing

Most modern newspapers are printed using a process called offset rotary printing on a rotary press. 'Offset' means that the printing plates do not touch the paper. 'Rotary' means that the cylinders carrying the printing plates spin round when the press is running.

The printing plates on each cylinder collect ink from an ink roller next to the cylinder. Ink only sticks to the parts of the plates that will form the printed pattern on the paper. Touching each plate-carrying cylinder is another cylinder, called a blanket cylinder, which is covered in rubber. The ink is transferred to the blanket cylinder, and then on to the paper. In colour units, each coloured ink is added one after the other.

These pages have been printed on different printing units and are on their way to the section of the press that cuts and folds them into finished newspapers.

ROLLING THE PRESS

By midnight, the **printing presses** begin to roll. A single press can produce an amazing 70,000 copies of a paper every hour. But the **print run** of a popular national daily newspaper can be several million, and all the papers need to be printed within a couple of hours, so several presses may need to work at once.

Once the press has started, it keeps going until all the newspapers have been printed. Even if a major story arrives just as the presses start, they have to carry on printing the whole print run; it takes too long to stop and re-start the press.

Newspaper paper

A newspaper press can use up to 50 tonnes of paper, called newsprint, every day. It comes on massive rolls about 2 metres high, weighing a tonne each. A roll, if completely unrolled, would be about 15 kilometres long! About half the paper that newspapers are printed on is made of recycled newspapers, which makes it cheap to buy.

Massive rolls of newsprint stored at a paper-making plant. One roll is being moved by a robot truck.

Rolls of paper are stored at the bottom of the press. Each one spins at high speed, feeding a continuous ribbon of paper called a web into the press. Each roll lasts about 20 minutes before it is empty. Just before one roll is finished, another roll is spun up to speed, and is automatically attached to the end of the previous roll.

Printing sheets

Most newspapers have some black pages and some colour. The paper goes through a mono unit first, where black text is printed on both sides. Then it goes to a colour unit, where colour pictures are added to one, or both, sides.

Quality control

Every few minutes, a **printing technician** examines a fresh newspaper to make sure that it has been printed properly. If the colours don't look right, the technician uses a computer linked to the press to adjust how much ink of each colour is being used.

A printing technician making a spot check on a freshly printed newspaper. Ear defenders protect his ears from the noise of the press.

DISTRIBUTION

The newspapers are carried straight from the **printing press** to the **distribution** department by conveyor belts. The press works so fast that dozens of newspapers arrive every second, so they must be cleared very quickly. Machines count the newspapers, stack them in piles, and tie the piles with plastic straps to make bundles. Each bundle is labelled with information about its destination and carried by conveyor belts to waiting lorries. Only a few minutes after the presses are started, the first lorries are on the road.

Most trucks go to local distribution centres, where the papers are loaded into vans and delivered to shops and news stands. Some newspapers are loaded on to trains for delivery to other areas. A few go by plane to other countries. By the time people are getting out of bed to go to school or work, their newspapers are dropping through their letterboxes. The stories inside them are being read often less than twelve hours after they were written.

It would be impossible for people to bundle up the newspapers fast enough to keep up with the printing press. Machines like the ones here do this job.

Bundles of finished newspapers being loaded into a truck to be transported to distribution centres, shops and news stands.

Remote printing

Many national newspapers are printed in several places around the country at the same time. This makes the printing and distribution much faster and more efficient. The completed pages of the paper are sent from computers at the newspaper's main office to computers at the other printing presses, where **printing plates** are made and printing is done. The information travels along high-speed communication lines only used for this purpose.

Selling papers

The number of copies of a newspaper that are sold is called its **circulation**. The higher the circulation, the more businesses will pay to advertise in the paper, and the more money the paper makes. The number of people who read the paper can be three or four times its circulation, as a household of several people might read a newspaper, but buy only one copy.

NEWS ON-LINE

Until the middle of the 1990s, the only way of reading newspaper stories was to buy a newspaper. But today, most national newspapers have **websites** on the **Internet** where the stories are published in electronic form. Anybody linked to the Internet can read the newspaper at any time of day.

The main advantage of publishing a newspaper on the Internet is that news stories can be added to the website as they happen. In a printed newspaper, they have to wait until the next day to be included in the next **edition**. There are other advantages too. **Editors** do not have to worry about cutting stories down to fit in small spaces on a page, and the stories can include sounds and video clips as well as photographs. News stories can be translated into different languages, which the reader can select before they start to read the paper. Many other **on-line** services, such as **search engines** and television companies, also publish news on the Internet.

A web page from an on-line newspaper. Breaking news stories can appear on a website as soon as they happen.

The Internet also makes producing printed newspapers easier. Reporters and photographers send **copy** and photographs to their offices by **e-mail**. Reporters and editors also find stories and check facts on the **World Wide Web**.

On-line news services will become more popular as people begin surfing the Internet through their televisions, palm-top computers and mobile phones. People will probably continue to buy traditional, printed newspapers, though, because they are cheap to buy and convenient to read anywhere.

Braille and speaking papers

A Braille newspaper is produced in Braille form for people with visual difficulties. Speaking newspapers are made up of recordings of people reading newspaper articles. People who have access to the Internet can use special software that converts the text on newspaper websites into speech.

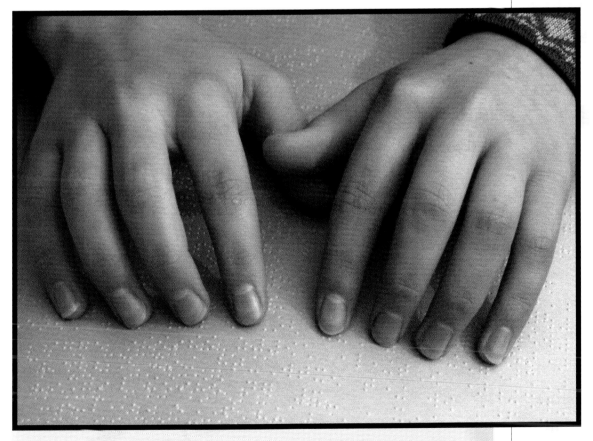

Braille is a series of raised bumps on the page. For each letter, the bumps are arranged differently and can be read by touch by a trained reader.

NEWSPAPER TIMELINE

Here are some of the major events and technical developments in the history of newspapers.

AD 100 The citizens of Ancient Rome can catch up with events in the Roman Senate by reading the *Acta diurna* (Daily Acts), which are stuck on a wall.

1100–1500 Merchants tell each other about daily events by circulating simple hand-written newsletters.

1440s A great breakthrough comes, when Johannes Gutenburg develops the **printing press**. He also develops type that can be moved around, which means that pages of text for printing can be made up by combining individual letters.

early 1600s The first recognizable newspapers appear both in northern Europe and Japan. At first they are just a single sheet of printed paper.

Print workers in New York in 1909. They are making up pages of metal type that will be used to print a newspaper. The same job is now done in a split second by computer.

This **edition** of the *Daily Mirror*, the first tabloid newspaper, was published on 14 April 1912. This was the day the famous passenger ship *Titanic* sank.

1690 The first American newspaper is published in Boston. It is called *Publick Occurrences Both Forreign and Domestick*, but lasts only for one issue.

1785 *The Times* of London is first published.

1800s High-speed rotary **presses** and automatic **typesetting** machines make newspaper printing far faster.

1851 *The New York Times* is first published. Paul Reuter starts a news service in London to provide foreign news to newspapers. The service is now known as Reuters (see page 9).

1903 The first tabloid (or half-sized newspaper) is published, called the *Daily Mirror*.

1970s **Page layout** software and computer typesetting make thousands of print workers jobless.

1998 Newspapers are first published on the **Internet**.

GLOSSARY

archive store of information for data that has been used before but that may be useful in the future

break refers to a story that comes into the news. The story is called a breaking story.

circulation number of copies of a particular newspaper that are sold every day or week

copy words that appear in a newspaper

database store of useful information on a computer that can be looked at by a person using the computer

digital 1) signal that is made up of on and off pulses of electricity, represented by the digits 0 and 1. 2) Any information stored in the form of the binary digits 0 and 1.

distribution sending packages from one place to many other places

download to copy a computer file from one computer to another computer

e-mail short for electronic mail, a system that allows people to send written messages to each other's computers via the Internet. Also the name given to a message.

edit to cut, add and move around words until they read correctly and take up the required space, or to choose pictures

editor person who chooses which stories and pictures to include in a newspaper, and who edits word or pictures

editorial column in a newspaper written by the editor or editor-in-chief which gives the opinion of the paper on current issues

edition one version of a newspaper

electronic picture desk computer where photographs for possible inclusion in a newspaper are stored and edited

feature regular section of a newspaper that appears every day or week, such as fashion or motoring sections

flat plan diagram of all the pages of a newspaper showing which features, articles and adverts will go where

freelance not employed by one company or organization, but working for several

graphics drawings, photographs and so on (in fact, everything except text) that appear in a newspaper

Internet global computer network that allows people with computers linked to it to access information on any other computer around the world, and to exchange e-mails with other people with computers

memory complex electronic circuits that remember digital information

modem device which allows a digital computer to be attached to an analogue telephone line

on-line connected to the Internet

page layout organizing and placing text and graphics on to the pages of a newspaper, normally using computers

print run number of copies of a newspaper that are printed in one go on a press

printing plate flat metal plate in a printing press with chemical patterns on it that collect ink and pass it on to the paper

printing press machine that presses patterns of ink on to paper to create newspapers or other documents

printing technician person who operates a printing press

printing unit section of a newspaper press that actually puts ink on the paper

proof copy of a page of a newspaper made before printing starts, to check that everything on the page looks correct

satellite object that orbits around the Earth in space

search engine special website that searches the Internet for other websites that you might be interested in

statistics records of numbers, such as the population of countries or the prices of items in shops

typesetting organizing metal, letter-shaped blocks (called type) into words and paragraphs for use in printing presses

upload to copy a computer file from your own computer to another, remote computer

website collection of information about a particular subject, stored on the Internet

World Wide Web also known as the Web, a huge source of information that can be accessed by any computer on the Internet

INDEX

Titles in the *Communicating Today* series:

Hardback   0 431 11375 0

Hardback   0 431 11370 X

Hardback   0 431 11374 2

Hardback   0 431 11371 8

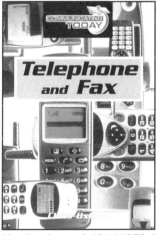

Hardback   0 431 11373 4

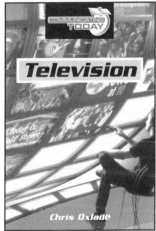

Hardback   0 431 11372 6

Find out about other Heinemann resources on our website www.heinemann.co.uk/library